DOMINIQUE NICOLE

Manifest You
BY DOMINIQUE NICOLE

CONTENTS

CHAPTER 1

THE DEFINITION OF MANIFESTATION

Hello Beautiful Humans...

You wouldn't believe how long it took me to do this.
It took me 20 years before I decided to sit down and allow the spirit of God to move through me and be still enough to write down my thoughts so I could deliver this message.

The time is NOW. It's time and that's also something that is amazingly beautiful about manifesting. Timing is everything.

In these 20 pages I want you to become a divine manifestor. Which is someone who creates the world that they want to see for themselves. To live and breath the life that your heart desires everyday. In order for me to be able to write this I had to do it for my self first. There will be a chapter that I will talk a little about my manifestation story. I believe it's truly why we go through certain things in life so that we pay attention to the steps so one day you will help someone else and if you are called to it help the world. Even if ONE LIFE changes for the better and they are able to have an amazing quality of life for them and their family. My heart will overflow with gratitude. Since that is what I desired all my life for me and my family.

The definition of manifestation: Let's define it spiritually first according to Google. "The public display of emotion or feeling, or something theoretical made real. Something spiritual becomes real."

Now let's define The God Manifestation: The Manifestations of God are appearances of the Divine Spirit or Holy Spirit in a series of personages, and as such, they perfectly reflect the attributes of the divine in to the human world for the progress and advancement of human morals and civilization through the agency of the same Spirit.

It's important to understand that we are bringing something that we see in the spirit into the natural into the physical world. Starting out let's look at science you have to believe first that we are all energy existing in a physical form. With understanding that it should bring you to a place of knowing that visualization is one of the main attributes to manifesting. Simply because you have to see it before it can exists.

CHAPTER 2

HOW TO MANIFEST

Let's take a deep dive into it right away. That's how I roll!!
I believe in getting straight to the point. Here are the
steps to start seeing your Life Visions come Alive to
Real Life Manifestation!

STEP 1: **Meditation**

Stillness is one of the most impactful and powerful pieces to everything in life.

Just hold on to that "**STILLNESS.**" This is where we receive so many answers from God the source of our existence. It's where we will hear and see as well as visualize all of what we want to become. Instead of calling someone on the phone take that time to just sit still close your eyes and listen for answers they will come and even if some of the ones that you want don't come at that moment LISTEN to the answers and the signs of what you DO, SEE, and HEAR in the STILLNESS. This is where you will develop everything that you are going to manifest. I literally could do a whole book on stillness. In stillness is where we restore and replenish our mind, body, and soul. In quietness there is a divine peace that will surpass all understanding. It will bring clarity to you within yourself. Clarity for your life. Visions and Answers develop and the sweet surrender starts to evolve. The sweet surrender of actually doing nothing, just allowing your spirit to align with the energy source of breath, the source of life, which is God Consciousness.

Set the scene for your stillness meditation. First thing in the morning go straight into your stillness and develop gratitude just being alive to have another day. To have a chance to be here on earth and do something amazing for yourself or someone. That's a divine spiritual manifestation in itself. I do my stillness practice 2 or 3 times a day. Another one of my favorite times of day is Sunset I call that the Golden Hour. There is a supremely divine energy manifesting at that time a day which energetically you can feel all of your prayers and visions and manifestations charging to come forth into the universe. Take advantage of the stillness in this magical hour of the day.

Light a candle and turn soothing music without words (instrumentals). This will help you to connect to vibration verses the words that someone else is saying. I love Dreamer Lounge by Estelle Blanca. After many years of practicing yoga I decided to become a certified yoga instructor and this has also evolved my practice of mediation and stillness. Yes I did say a practice, believe me repetition will become your new friend. We are creatures of habit so whatever we do over and over again becomes who we are. Since we are spiritual energy in existence our energy connects to what we do, what we say, and ultimately who we are. All of this energy comes together and creates your divine presence. The more you do anything you fill your mind, body, and soul up with it.

STEP 2: **Rewiring Your Brain**

You literally have to spend time reprogramming your mind. The way that your life got into the space and condition that it is in today ALL has to do with how you think. So first take responsibility for that yourself and don't blame anyone or anything. OWN IT. Taking the time to reprogram how you think is powerful. You have to become your own professional guru of your thought life. Take a look at how you are looking at things. Perspective is everything. If your finances are running out too quickly look at how you are spending. Start seeing large sums of money in your bank account and realistically figure out a way to start saving to get there. Imagine 10k as your daily running balance and then grow from there to 20k and 30k etc. Come up with ways to increase your income products, or services.

STEP 3: **Repetition**

Daily repetition: Start listening to things in repetition with focus on the things that you want to see in your life. Tune into my Utube Channel dominiquenicole. I'm simply repeating our main areas of life that we have to tune into in life to receive abundance. LOVE MONEY PEACE and SELF CARE. Repetition is one of my favorite words in the world. Because anything you repeat over and over you will become. It simply starts to download into your subconscious mind and then it develops into a thought and the thought becomes a force of energy, which then is something you have to decide on doing. You either take action on it or it flows back into the subconscious pool or it becomes action. This is something I learned with my television and film career with character development. An exercise that we would literally do is people watch and come back and practice what we saw people do. Then we would visualize it and connect to the conversation and repeat. So powerful! Pretty soon you will become the character in the scene and you are living the life of that person. A divine key is not to loose yourself your personality your uniqueness is so important its something special just about how you do it.

CHAPTER 3

WHY YOU ARE SO DIVINE

Let me just tell you something very bluntly. There is only ONE you! We only get 1 of YOU. YOU ARE DIVINELY and SUPREMELY SPECIAL AND UNIQUE. Every single life on this earth has purpose. It's doesn't matter how many people are doing what you are about to do. It doesn't matter if you see things or people out there doing it in a different way. Hold on tight to your vision and manifest exactly what you see. That is your mission. It's okay if the mission changes hold on to each aspect of it sometimes the visualizations of it comes in bits and pieces and you have to write it down in a journal so you can look back and put it together until you see exactly what it is. That is what Steve Jobs was talking about when he said to connect the dots. Live happens moment-by-moment and day-by-day be patient take time to watch it unfold and come together. This is why we have to manifest things on our own. It's amazing to do the process with someone but you have to understand that their thoughts and ideas are now included in your vision. That's why when you are in the mediation process the alone time with stillness gives you clarity perfectly and uniquely for you. Now when you include your partner, friend, husband, or wife remember to go into the mediation on what you are going to focus on together so your energies will align. That way there's more power manifesting. That's why the relationship should be highly connected spiritually and be very like minded with that person because you don't want anything to block what you are processing to bring forth. That's why I have to let you know how uniquely divine You Are. Believe me when I say No One Can Do It Like You.

CHAPTER 4

MY STORY OF MANIFESTATION

I'm a Midwest girl from St. Louis Missouri. I came from humble beginnings. We were a middle class family and I was raised of the Catholic Faith. I was taught to always follow the rules. Even though every Nun that was in my life was amazing and a truly divine blessing to me. I have realized sometimes you got to do what you are feeling in your soul even if the so called rules don't tell you to do so. If you just follow all rules 1 by 1 you will miss the opportunity to create. I have learned that the rules are the foundation and they help you build. So I'm so thankful for every teacher and supporter of my education. One thing for sure is that you do need to learn how to color in the lines. I must say I also have learned you have to learn how to make your own lines and develop your own color or even your own first flower. BE THE CREATOR "Calmative, First Flower" is also a song I love to be creative with. That music stimulates my creative brain waves. It's amazing... In music there is so many moments and beats that connect to emotions and creativity that's why I always suggest to create the scene. Your environment has a lot of energy in it so make your stillness mediation area very serene and inviting warm as well as tranquil. FYI Don't worry about the so called mistakes they do not exist sometimes that is where some of the most magical manifestations happen the God moments of what's not even thought of or seen! Since my life had so much structure and my acting career was so much fun I figured out that I needed to find some ways to boost my income so I could create the life that I truly wanted. So I went into Corporate America it taught me a lot and talk about structure oh my goodness if you stay in Corporate you might become a robot. You totally can loose yourself just doing things that people tell you to do all day everyday. Even in Corporate find a way to be creative just so you stay in tune with the creative process which I believe is the reason we are all here to be CREATORS. I suggest to learn all of the systems and operations in any job that you have. In order to truly create your world you have to be willing to take a leap of faith so that you can live each and every day the way your spirit guides you. Now every person isn't meant to be an Entrepreneur but as an Artist my self I say there isn't anything better than in manifesting your vision and becoming in business for yourself. The empowerment it gives you to be a CEO puts the crown of leadership on you and places a divine power inside of you to give you the energy like a force of divine nature to fulfill your purpose. Cross the bridge! MANIFEST THE LIFE YOU WANT.

CHAPTER 5

KEEP GOING

In life you will go through many processes.
In this world system success is measured by results.
Organizations do not give the cycle of repetition a place.
We all were taught that repetition was a bad thing.

When really the repetition of any process or success or system will take you into many depths and focus of that one thing. Which makes you a master of that thing! That's explosive information in order to Master anything you do it over and over again to gain new perspective and grow as well as gain depth in what you already know that is called evolving .

No matter what you are doing go deep. Do not be concerned about how long you have been doing it. Right when you get ready to leave it or turn to something new would be the season and time that you will break through to new dimensions and levels in that area. So Keeping Going!

I love the quote "Success is when preparation meets opportunity."

No matter how long you are working on something you are constantly in a place of preparation. When you are working in one area for any amount of time you have an opportunity to experience different ways of doing that one thing which gives you new dimensions of perspective so you can communicate on many different levels on this one subject. This is extremely powerful! This will allow you to be able to reach many different people and which is the foundation of every purpose. To reach many different people with what you have inside of you should be your ultimate foundational goal.

It is excellent to measure what you are doing by the results that you have made but do not stop there. If the progress that you thought that you should have had has not happened yet keep going. No matter what keep going anyway that way you always have chance to find out something new.

It is also excellent to set goals so you can celebrate your accomplishments along the way. There is a place and reason for everything!

These goals are great ways to make sure you stay on course of your plan but life also has it's own rhythm so flow. Yes go with the flow like Bruce Lee move like water.

You have the opportunity to live a life with no limits!

Be willing to go beyond where you have before. Be willing to go when everyone has stopped.

The better the focus the better the aim and the more power and energy you will have so that you can hit your target and manifest.

When you decide to take the road that is least followed. Doors will open for you that no one else has seen or touched that were divinely set for you. This is where you will establish new ways of doing many different things for this one thing, which gives you an elevated mind, and thought processes.

KEEP GOING...

Keep going and stay true to your plan

Keep going even when no one understands

Keep going because you will learn how to be more true to you

Keep going even when you may not no what to do

Keep going because the vision you have will manifest dreams

Keep going even when your running low and you have to console yourself and replenish your self-esteem

Keep going because the other side is not far away

Keep going because this is the place where Successful Leaders are made

Keep going because you don't want to leave this earth with your music and story inside of you

Keep going because your assignment and story can only be delivered by you!

I encourage everyone to keep going and do not look back continue to press forward to complete your purpose and assignment that is on your life. No one can do anything like you. You are a divinely designed by the one and only original spiritual force GOD.

— By Dominique Nicole

DOMINIQUE NICOLE

THOUGHTS

THOUGHTS

THOUGHTS

THOUGHTS

BELIEFS

BELIEFS

BELIEFS

BELIEFS

BELIEFS

VISION

VISION

VISION

VISION

VISION

MANIFESTATIONS

MANIFESTATIONS

MANIFESTATIONS

MANIFESTATIONS

MANIFESTATIONS

DOMINIQUE NICOLE

▶ DOMINIQUENICOLE

f DOMINIQUENICOLETV

🟥 DOMINIQUENICOLETV

🐦 DNFILMS

🌐 DNICOLEYOGA.COM

✉ BOOKING@DOMINIQUENICOLE.COM

ISBN 978-0-578-72242-9

90000>

9 780578 722429

www.ingramcontent.com/pod-product-compliance
Lightning Source LLC
Chambersburg PA
CBHW061050090426
42740CB00002B/101